BOYS' LIFE

A COMEDY
BY HOWARD KORDER

DRAMATISTS
PLAY SERVICE
INC.

SPECIAL NOTE

Anyone receiving permission to produce BOY'S LIFE is required to give credit to the Author as sole and exclusive Author of the Play on the title page of all programs distributed in connection with performances of the Play and in all instances in which the title of the Play appears for purposes of advertising, publicizing or otherwise exploiting the Play and/or a production thereof. The name of the Author must appear on a separate line, in which no other name appears, immediately beneath the title and in size of type equal to 50% of the size of the largest, most prominent letter used for the title of the Play. No person, firm or entity may receive credit larger or more prominent than that accorded the Author.

SPECIAL NOTE ON SONGS AND RECORDINGS

For performances of copyrighted songs, arrangements or recordings mentioned in this Play, the permission of the copyright owner(s) must be obtained. Other songs, arrangements or recordings may be substituted provided permission from the copyright owner(s) of such songs, arrangements or recordings is obtained; or songs, arrangements or recordings in the public domain may be substituted.

SPECIAL NOTE ON ORIGINAL MUSIC

A CD (#1092CD) with cue sheet containing the original music composed by David Yazbek for the New York production of this Play is available through the Play Service for $28.00, which includes packing and regular shipping. The fee for the use of this music is $10.00 per performance.

For Lois

BOYS' LIFE was presented by Lincoln Center Theater (Gregory Mosher, Director; Bernard Gersten, Executive Producer) at the Mitzi E. Newhouse theater in New York City, opening on February 29, 1988. The Atlantic Theater Company was directed by W. H. Macy; the sets were by James Wolk; the costumes were by Donna Zakowska; the lighting was by Steve Lawnick; the sound was by Aural Fixation; the original music was composed by David Yazbek; the production manager was Jeff Hamlin; the general manager was Steve C. Callahan; the general press agent was Merle Debuskey; and the production stage manager was Thomas A. Kelly. The cast, in order of appearance, was as follows:

DON	Jordan Lage
PHIL	Steven Goldstein
JACK	Clark Gregg
KAREN	Mary McCann
MAN	Todd Weeks
MAGGIE	Felicity Huffman
LISA	Melissa Bruder
GIRL	Robin Spielberg
CARLA	Théo Cohan

CHARACTERS
JACK
DON
PHIL

A MAN

LISA
MAGGIE
KAREN
GIRL
CARLA

All in their late twenties

TIME
The present.
Various intervals over the course of a year.

PLACE
A large city.

BOYS' LIFE

SCENE 1

Don's bedroom. Jack smoking a joint. Phil lying on the floor, wearing a set of headphones. Don sitting in his underwear. Bottles, clothes, books scattered on the floor. 1 A.M.

JACK. Remember the nineteen-seventies?
DON. Sure. Sort of.
JACK. Name three things that happened in the nineteen-seventies.
DON. This is like a trick question, right?
JACK. I'll give you one minute.
PHIL. (*Loudly, tapping phones.*) I haven't heard this since *col*lege, you know?
JACK. (*Smiling and nodding.*) Eat me, Phil.
PHIL. (*Not hearing.*) Okay!
JACK. Give up?
DON. That wasn't a minute.
JACK. Let's go.
PHIL. *Great* bass line.
DON. Um . . .
JACK. Do it!
DON. Um . . . Watergate? And . . . uh . . . (*Pause.*) The Sex Pistols . . . and . . . uh . . . (*Pause.*) Did I say Watergate?
JACK. I rest my case.
DON. Ah . . . giant leap for a man?
JACK. Oh, hang it *up*, Don.
DON. Did I *say* Watergate?
JACK. You're losing it, Don. Your mind is going.
DON. The nineteen-seventies.
JACK. You're rotting on the vine.
PHIL. (*Imitating an electric guitar.*) War-raaang! (*Pause.*)
JACK. Well, *I'm* having fun.

5

DON. Me too.

JACK. I know you are. We live in thrilling days, Don.

DON. We *do.*

JACK. And I think that's swell.

DON. I do too.

JACK. I know you do. You're an agreeable guy. And I've been meaning to tell you this, really, if someone came up to me and asked, "Now this *Don* fellow, what's he all about?" I'd have to tell him, well, darn it, Don, Don's an *agreeable* guy.

DON. I'd go along with that.

JACK. Would you go along with a toast?

DON. (*Picking up a beer.*) By all means.

JACK. To you, Don, for being the postmodern kind of nut you are.

DON. Thanks, Jack.

JACK. To Phil, a great guy in spite of some desperate handicaps.

PHIL. (*Not hearing.*) Okay!

JACK. And to me, for being perfect.

DON. Not easy.

JACK. And Don, to our times together. From campus cut-ups to wasted potentials.

DON. It feels like years.

JACK. It *has* been years.

DON. We are getting old.

JACK. To our parents, Don. To the dream they called America. To the Big Kidder upstairs. To, ah . . .

PHIL. (*Imitating drums.*) Da-dum-dum-dum-dum-*dum* . . .

DON. The ladies!

JACK. Don, a toast, a very *special* toast, to the ladies.

DON. Oh my.

JACK. Yes indeed. Where would we be without them?

DON. We'd be nowhere.

JACK. We wouldn't be *here.*

DON. We wouldn't even *exist.*

JACK. We would not.

DON. It's a sobering thought.

JACK. It's food for thought.

DON. It's a thought to think. (*Pause.*)

JACK. Well, no sense in blaming them for it now.
DON. It's a dead issue.
JACK. It's all said and done. Cause when you come right down to it . . .
PHIL. I *love* this part . . .
JACK. A man . . .
DON. Is a *man*.
JACK. He *is* a man.
DON. By *any* other name.
JACK. He'd still smell.
DON. Amen.
JACK. God*damn*.
DON. Goddamn *shit*.
JACK. *Cocksucking* shit.
DON. Goddamn shiteating asshole *scumbags*! (*Jack breaks out into a wolf howl. Don joins in. Pause.*) You know, you'd never have this kind of talk with a woman.
JACK. No, you wouldn't. And I want you always to remember this, Don. When you're old and pissing in your daybed, remember who brought you out of the jungle and shaved off your fur.
DON. (*In a zombie-like monotone.*) It was you master. You teach Don to walk like man.
JACK. And you *better* be grateful. (*He drags on the joint.*) Here. Finish that off. Come on, come on. (*He passes the joint to Don. Don takes a hit. Silence. He smiles.*) What are you smiling about?
DON. Nah, I was just thinking.
JACK. Uh-huh.
DON. I used to really want to be an astronaut, you know? Be up there. The quiet. Walter Cronkite talking about me to millions of people. But I wouldn't have to *listen*.
JACK. So?
DON. So I'd still like to be an astronaut.
JACK. Maybe you will be, Don. But even if you were . . . you'd still have to get out of bed in the morning.
DON. (*Thinking it over.*) Yeah. (*Pause. Phil takes off the headphones.*)
PHIL. Emerson, Lake, and Palmer, man, whatever happened to them?

7

JACK. They all died horribly, Phil, in a bus crash.
PHIL. They did? That's really depressing.
JACK. I thought it might be. (*Pause.*) Well, gentlemen. Anybody have a good fuck lately?
PHIL. Does masturbation count? (*Blackout.*)

SCENE 2

A child's bedroom. Phil and Karen standing at opposite ends of the room, facing each other. The bed is piled with coats. Sounds of a party filter in from outside.

PHIL. Well, there *you* are.
KAREN. Yes.
PHIL. And here I am.
KAREN. Yes.
PHIL. So here we are, both of us. Together.
KAREN. Talking.
PHIL. Right here in the same room.
KAREN. It's pretty amazing. (*Pause.*) Enjoying the party?
PHIL. Oh, yes. Certainly. Yes yes yes.
KAREN. Mmmm.
PHIL. No.
KAREN. Oh.
PHIL. Not in the larger sense.
KAREN. Why did you come?
PHIL. I was invited. I mean . . . Jack invited me.
KAREN. And you do everything Jack says.
PHIL. No, I . . . he's my friend. My oldest friend. (*Pause.*) You look great tonight, Karen.
KAREN. Thanks.
PHIL. No, I mean it. Just wonderful. (*Pause.*)
KAREN. You look good.
PHIL. No.
KAREN. You do.
PHIL. No I don't.
KAREN. Really, you do.
PHIL. Do I?
KAREN. What do you want, Phil?

8

PHIL. Well, I don't *want* anything. I just wanted to . . . say hello.

KAREN. Hello.

PHIL. Yes, well. (*Pause.*) That's lovely, what you have on, what is it?

KAREN. A dress.

PHIL. I've always admired your sense of humor, Karen.

KAREN. What do you want, Phil? (*The door opens and a man pops his head in.*)

MAN. Oh. I'm sorry.

KAREN. We're almost done.

MAN. Oh. Well. Fine. I'll, ah . . . fine. (*He exits, closing the door.*)

PHIL. What was that all about?

KAREN. What?

PHIL. That. That guy.

KAREN. I don't know.

PHIL. Well, you seemed pretty familiar with him.

KAREN. Are you feeling okay?

PHIL. Hmm? Oh, sure. Things are going really really great for me right now. Just fine. I have my own partition now, over at the office, they put up one of those, ah . . . so *that's* really good. And I'm going to the spa a lot, I'm working ou—well, I can't use the machines cause you know of my back, but I love the Jacuzzi, so, actually, it's strange, cause I fell asleep in it, in the whirlpool, and when I woke up I had this incredible headache, I mean it would *not* go away, I felt this thing here like the size of a peach pit, I went for a *blood* test, I was convinced I, you hear all this stuff now, the way it's spreading, I mean I'm not—but I was sure I had it.

KAREN. Had what?

PHIL. It. You know. (*Pause.*)

KAREN. And?

PHIL. I didn't. So. (*Pause. Karen looks at the door.*) Anyway, it's funny we both happened to turn up here tonight, isn't it, cause I was just thinking, I was wondering . . . I mean, it's a couple of months since I last spoke to you and I was just *wondering* if we were still, you know, seeing each other.

KAREN. *Seeing* each other.

PHIL. Yes.

KAREN. No. (*Pause.*)

PHIL. All right.

KAREN. We were never seeing each other, Phil.

PHIL. Well, no, not actually *seeing* . . .

KAREN. We slept together once.

PHIL. Twice.

KAREN. You left before I woke up.

PHIL. Okay, Yeah, but . . . I mean, *everybody* does that.

KAREN. And you never called.

PHIL. Now . . . now about *that*, you see, I was involved in a very bad kind of situation then, and I wasn't really in a position to, ah . . . as much as I *wanted* to . . . and I *did*, very, very—

KAREN. What do you want?

PHIL. (*Pause.*) Well, I'd like another shot at it.

KAREN. At what?

PHIL. At you. To get to know you.

KAREN. I'm really not worth the effort, Phil.

PHIL. You're seeing someone else, right?

KAREN. That's got nothing to—

PHIL. You *are* seeing someone.

KAREN. Not actually *seeing* . . .

PHIL. No, no, it's fine. Early bird and all that stuff. I'm fine. Everything is fine.

KAREN. It's got nothing to do with you, Phil. There's just a lot of things I have to work through right now. But I like you, I do. You're . . . you're a wonderful person.

PHIL. You're a wonderful person too, Karen.

KAREN. Well, so are you, Phil.

PHIL. That's right. We both are. (*He hugs Karen.*) Listen to this. A guy in my office has a cabin upstate. He never uses it. It's on the edge of a beautiful freshwater lake. Why don't we go there, just the two of us, we spend the weekend, relax, get out of the city . . . do some straight thinking. What do you say?

KAREN. No.

PHIL. Is it because of this guy you're seeing?

KAREN. Well, I'm not actually *seeing*—

PHIL. Then what is it?

KAREN. It's just not a good idea.

PHIL. It's not?

KAREN. No. Not at all. (*Pause.*) You're touching my breasts, Phil. (*The man pops his head through the door.*)

MAN. Oh gosh. Beg pardon. (*He shuts the door.*)

PHIL. I think about you a lot, Karen.

KAREN. You do.

PHIL. Yes. At work, you know, the laundromat, in the shower . . . places like that. (*Pause.*) I mean that in the positive sense.

KAREN. I'm not worth the trouble.

PHIL. It's just two days out of your life, Karen. This could turn out to be something really special, it'll be over before you know it.

KAREN. You're making this very difficult.

PHIL. I'm making it incredibly *easy*. Come up to the country with me.

KAREN. Phil—

PHIL. Come.

KAREN. Please, Phil—

PHIL. I'm asking for a *chance*.

KAREN. Oh, no. Oh no. This is coming at a very bad time for me. I don't think I can handle this right now. My life is a real big mess, okay, and . . . I read that by the time you're five you've already developed the major patterns for the rest of your life. I mean whether you're going to be basically happy or . . . a fireman, a lesbian, whatever. And of course it's not fair at all, because nobody tells a little kid anything about that. But that's the way it is. So I've been thinking about this. And it occurs to me that somewhere along the line I screwed up really bad. I made a very poor choice about something and now there's nothing I can do to change it.

PHIL. I think I love you.

KAREN. You haven't even been listening.

PHIL. Of course I have. You were talking about your childhood, right? I love you.

KAREN. No, Phil. I'm really very flattered—

PHIL. I'm not saying it to flatter you, Karen. We're not talking about your drapes. We're talking about this very real and undeniable feeling I have for you. So you're not

11

happy. I think I can sense that from what you just told me. But *nobody's* happy. That's the way things are *supposed* to be. You think I'm happy? I'm not happy, I'm miserable.

KAREN. I am too.

PHIL. I know you are. That's why I feel so close to you. Karen? I can *make* you happy. And you can make me happy. We can help each other.

KAREN. You just said that nobody is happy.

PHIL. I didn't *mean* that. I feel so crazy when I'm with you I don't know what I'm saying. I love you.

KAREN. No—please—

PHIL. I love you. I'm sick with needing you. It's an actual disease. I'm all swollen and rotten inside, my brain is decomposing, and it's because of you.

KAREN. What's wrong with you, Phil?

PHIL. I'm dying without you, Karen. I'm serious. Has anyone ever told you anything like that? Ever?

KAREN. No. Never.

PHIL. Because no one has ever loved you as much as I do. Jesus, Karen, help me! (*The man pops his head through the door.*)

MAN. Excuse me . . .

PHIL. What? What do you want?

MAN. Well . . . my coat . . .

PHIL. In a minute.

MAN. I've been waiting—

PHIL. GO AWAY! (*The man shuts the door.*) I love you.

KAREN. For how long?

PHIL. Until I'm in my grave. Longer. Forever.

KAREN. No, I mean . . . how long would we have to be away for?

PHIL. As long as you want. We don't even have to come back.

KAREN. I was thinking just the weekend.

PHIL. Yes, yes, the weekend. A day. An hour. A single second.

KAREN. I have pasta class Monday nights.

PHIL. Great. Fabulous. (*Pause.*)

KAREN. I wish I could, Phil. It's not that I don't want to . . .

12

PHIL. If you want to, just say yes. Don't worry about the rest.

KAREN. I can't.

PHIL. Then just say maybe.

KAREN. If I say maybe, you'll think I'm saying yes.

PHIL. I won't. I promise. I'm very clear on maybe. (*Pause.*) Please, Karen. Give me a crumb. Throw me a line.

KAREN. Oh, let me think about it, I have to . . . okay. Maybe. I'd like to—I don't know, maybe.

PHIL. Maybe. Maybe. Thank you, Karen. You won't be sorry. I'm crazy about you. You know that, don't you?

KAREN. I'm not worth it, Phil. Really.

PHIL. This is the happiest day of my life. (*He kisses her and eases her down onto the bed. He climbs on top of her and starts to caress her. The man enters.*)

MAN. Look, I'm very sorry about this, but I need my coat. (*Karen breaks away and sits on the edge of the bed.*) Sorry.

KAREN. That's all right. We're done.

MAN. Are you?

PHIL. (*Rising from the bed.*) Come on. Let's get back to the party.

KAREN. No, you go ahead.

PHIL. You're not coming?

KAREN. In a minute.

PHIL. (*Moving toward her.*) Is everything okay?

KAREN. Yes, yes, it's really—Phil, no please, please, just stay away—(*To the man.*) Look, I'm sorry, I—(*Turning away.*) Oh God I hate myself so *much*! (*She runs out of the room.*)

PHIL. (*Following her.*) Karen, wait a—(*She slams the door.*) Shit. Shit shit shit! (*He leans against the door. Silence.*)

MAN. Interesting girl, isn't she? In her way?

PHIL. Huh?

MAN. Personality-wise.

PHIL. How would you know?

MAN. She was sort of my date.

PHIL. Oh.

MAN. But I don't think it's gonna work out. High-strung, you know? I got better things to do. (*Pause.*)

PHIL. We're in love.

13

MAN. You and her?
PHIL. Yes.
MAN. Congratulations.
PHIL. Thanks. (*Pause.*)
MAN. You want to reimburse me for cab fare or what?
(*Blackout*)

SCENE 3

Lights up on Jack and Maggie sitting on a bench opposite a playground in a city park. Jack smokes a joint. Maggie, wheezing heavily, wears a motley exercise suit with race number tied around her chest below a small pin-on button. She has a pair of headphones in her ears.

MAGGIE. Oh God. Oh God.
JACK. Been doing some running, huh? (*Pause. Maggie pays him no attention.*) Hey. (*Maggie turns to him.*) Out doing some *running*, huh? (*Maggie taps her headphones, smiles curtly, and turns away.*) *Excuse* me. (*He taps her shoulder.*)
MAGGIE. What?
JACK. I'm talking to you.
MAGGIE. Yes?
JACK. Asked you a question?
MAGGIE. What?
JACK. What's it *for*?
MAGGIE. Huh?
JACK. The race.
MAGGIE. We're jogging against apartheid.
JACK. Really.
MAGGIE. No. Of course not.
JACK. Oh. (*Pause.*) Interesting people, the Boers, you think?
MAGGIE. I wouldn't know. (*Pause. Maggie coughs violently.*)
JACK. Something wrong?
MAGGIE. I'm going to die.
JACK. You should catch your breath.
MAGGIE. What I'm trying to *do*.
JACK. (*Noticing the button on her chest.*) May I? (*He leans in*

14

closely.) Ah yes. "Question Authority."
MAGGIE. That's what it says.
JACK. You know—excuse me—that's a bad place for a button. It can restrict your circulation, should I take it off?
MAGGIE. Where'd you get that?
JACK. I beg your pardon, but I didn't "get it" anywhere. It's something I have to know in my line of work.
MAGGIE. And what might that be?
JACK. I'm a cardiologist. (*Pause.*)
MAGGIE. Please go away.
JACK. Pardon?
MAGGIE. You heard me. I'm not in the mood for it. Go bother somebody else. (*Pause. Jack looks at her and turns away. Silence. Suddenly he leaps up.*)
JACK. (*Out.*) HEY, JASON! YO! *OFF* THE SWINGS! . . . YEAH, THAT'S RIGHT! (*Pause.*) I'LL COME OVER THERE! I'LL COME OVER THERE! YOU WANT ME TO COME O—(*Pause. He sits.*) Kid's looking for a brick in the head.
MAGGIE. Cute.
JACK. Yah.
MAGGIE. How old?
JACK. I dunno . . . five, six maybe.
MAGGIE. You don't know how old your kid is?
JACK. Hey. He's not *mine.*
MAGGIE. Sorry, it—
JACK. What do I look like? Come *on.*
MAGGIE. *Okay.*
JACK. I wouldn't have a kid like that. Give me some credit. (*Pause.*) He's my ward.
MAGGIE. Your ward.
JACK. Well, I'm more like his tutor.
MAGGIE. What do you teach him?
JACK. What do I *teach* him? I *teach* him about *life.* Don't play with matches . . . write down phone messages . . . that kind of thing. (*Pause.*) Ah, sorry I bothered you. I didn't mean to bother you.
MAGGIE. Yeah, well.
JACK. It's just you looked . . . in need.
MAGGIE. I'm not. (*Pause.*) What's ten k?

15

JACK. Pardon?

MAGGIE. Ten k, what is it?

JACK. Well, I think it comes to around six miles.

MAGGIE. Miles.

JACK. It's, you know, metric.

MAGGIE. Six *miles*? I'm gonna kill him.

JACK. Who?

MAGGIE. Nobody. A friend.

JACK. Must be quite a fella.

MAGGIE. He's an asshole. You know?

JACK. Sure. (*He offers her the joint.*) You want?

MAGGIE. No. Yes. (*She takes it.*) What am I doing? What am I doing?

JACK. Well, it looks to me like—JASON! OVER HERE! WHAT ARE YOU, AN IDIOT? HOW MANY TIMES AM I GONNA TELL YOU? STOP ACTING LIKE A MONGOLOID AND GET OFF THE SWING! (*Pause.*) WHAT? WHAT DID YOU SAY? (*Pause.*) THAT'S *RIGHT* YOU SAID NOTHING! Let me tell you, that kid has a mouth like a sewer. I don't know where he gets it from. *I'd* have that kid horsewhipped. You can't do that though, can you? They're delicate, aren't they? There are all kinds of sociological factors involved. You smack them in the head, next thing you know they're strolling through Arby's with a high-powered rifle. And you're to blame.

MAGGIE. Come on.

JACK. You think I'm kidding? Nine out of ten experts will agree with me. Have another hit.

MAGGIE. I shouldn't. (*She takes the joint. They look at each other. Pause.*)

JACK. What's on the phones?

MAGGIE. Oh, nothing.

JACK. It's okay, I'm eclectic. Fred Waring Singers?

MAGGIE. No, it's nothing. Actual nothing. They're not plugged in, see? (*Pause.*) You know how sometimes you just can't stand to talk to someone? You know?

JACK. Your friend.

MAGGIE. It's not enough he's prancing around in spandex pajamas, he's got to keep telling me how *wonderful* it feels to be *alive* on a day like this. And how he feels all this energy,

16

this *beautiful* energy *flowing* out of him. He's like a cheap microwave.

JACK. Spandex pajamas?

MAGGIE. It's his outfit. He's got all these . . . *outfits*, right? He never just *wears* anything. (*Pause.*) Listen.

JACK. Yes.

MAGGIE. He gets his body waxed. I'm not kidding.

JACK. Well.

MAGGIE. Not a hair on him. He's from Portugal.

JACK. Right.

MAGGIE. So there you have it. (*Pause.*) Your kid's on the monkey bars, is that okay?

JACK. He's not my kid.

MAGGIE. Well, your whatever. Christ, I'm stoned. (*She giggles.*) You're not really a cardiologist.

JACK. Not literally, no.

MAGGIE. So are you trying to pick me up or what?

JACK. I'm just sitting here.

MAGGIE. You sit here often?

JACK. I've got a lot of quality time on my hands. (*Pause.*) HEY! WHAT I SAY ABOUT HANGING UPSIDE DOWN, HUH? REMEMBER JUSTIN HENRY!

MAGGIE. Who?

JACK. That punk from *Kramer Vs. Kramer.* You know where he falls off the jungle gym? I made him watch it on the VCR. Now he wants to be in the movies, are you seriously involved?

MAGGIE. Where?

JACK. Your Portuguese friend.

MAGGIE. Yeah, sure. We bought a sofa bed together. That counts for something, doesn't it, we both sleep on it. (*Pause.*) Ah, my god. He loves me, and I can't listen to him speak without looking for the carving knife. He's so . . . I mean, just what is going *on*? What are we *doing*? We drift into record shops, we wear nice clothes, we eat Cajun food, and what is all that? It's *garbage*, that's all it really is. Absolute . . . Where's the foundation, eh? Where's the . . . Look, I read the papers. He doesn't know it. The world is coming to an end. I'm not *kidding*. We need to be getting better, don't we? As a species? We should be improving. But we're not. The world is coming to an end and I'm spending my last moments thinking about . . . ach, who *knows*, sugar cones, skin cream, *nonsense*. Do you follow me?

JACK. Yes. Yes, I—

MAGGIE. I don't want to help other people. I say I do but I don't. I wish they would go away. Why doesn't that bother me? I don't know. I don't know. (*Pause.*)

JACK. Great dope, huh?

MAGGIE. Yeah. (*Silence.*)

JACK. You ever see *It's a Wonderful Life?*

MAGGIE. No.

JACK. It's on TV all the time.

MAGGIE. I haven't seen it. It's not a crime.

JACK. Okay, Jimmy Stewart wants to kill himself, right? He's gonna jump off a bridge. Then this angel, bear with me, angel comes down, shows what the world would have been like if he'd never lived. And Jimmy Stewart realizes all the good he's done, without even knowing it.

MAGGIE. Uh-huh.

JACK. Didn't even *know* it.

MAGGIE. So . . . what good have you done?

JACK. Well, there you go. I might be another Mother Theresa, who can say?

MAGGIE. Or you might just be selfish.

JACK. Yeah, that's another possibility. (*Pause.*) I'm going to be finished here pretty soon.

MAGGIE. How nice for you.

JACK. Maybe we could get together.

MAGGIE. How do you mean?

JACK. You know, get . . . together. See what happens. I'm not trying to pick you up.

MAGGIE. What are you trying to do?

JACK. We could just talk. (*Pause.*) Would you like to talk? I think we could talk about some things. (*Pause.*) Listen. I want to talk to you. (*Pause.*)

MAGGIE. What about your ward?

JACK. I'll drop him off.

MAGGIE. Where?

JACK. Where he *lives*.

MAGGIE. And where is that? (*Pause.*)

JACK. Well . . . (*Pause.*) It would be interesting, wouldn't it?

MAGGIE. Yes. Very. But that's really not a *reason*. Besides . . . you're married.

JACK. No I'm not.

MAGGIE. And you've got a kid.

JACK. No, I don't.

MAGGIE. And I think you're just kind of stoned and bored. (*Pause.*) Sorry. (*Silence. Jack stares out.*)

JACK. Look at that kid. I swear he's living with his head up his ass.

MAGGIE. Maybe he'll become a proctologist.

JACK. Yah.

MAGGIE. I'm Maggie.

JACK. Jack. Hello, Maggie.

MAGGIE. Hello, Jack.

JACK. Hi. (*Maggie starts out, turns back.*)

MAGGIE. Um . . . (*She looks at him. Pause. She shakes her head and exits. Jack watches her go. Silence. He looks at his watch.*)

JACK. ALL RIGHT, JASON, HAUL IT IN, TIME'S UP . . . HEY, DID YOU HEAR ME? I SAID HAUL IT IN! JASON, YOU GET OVER HERE PRONTO OR I'M GONNA DECK YOU, UNDERSTAND? DADDY'S GONNA BREAK YOUR LITTLE HEINIE! I'M GONNA COUNT TO FIVE, JASON. ONE . . . TWO . . . THREE . . . (*Pause.*) FOUR . . . (*Pause.*) ALL RIGHT, THAT'S IT. I'M CALLING MOMMY! (*Blackout.*)

SCENE 4

Lights up. Don and Lisa sitting at a table in a restaurant.

DON. Would you like another drink?

LISA. No. (*Pause.*) Do you understand what I mean?

DON. Uh-huh.

LISA. So why do they do it?

DON. I don't know.

LISA. Like these men going around with all this, what,

19

military shit, you know, zippers everywhere, combat boots, flak jackets, I mean people *died* in those things. And their heads, they tilt their heads back, just a little, looking down at you like, "Hey, baby, you like this? I'm *dangerous*. Don't *fuck* with me." Who are they *kidding*? Those people, I mean *really dangerous* people, they don't look like that. They laugh at people like that. "Hey baby." Come on.

DON. Sure.

LISA. And you see them in the stores, or they're getting their *hair* cut, going, "I want to look like so and so, you know, like a rock star, or a *killer*." Right? Like a *killer*. Why *is* that? Why do they want to look like that?

DON. You mean those guys?

LISA. Yes.

DON. I don't know.

LISA. Do they think it's attractive?

DON. I don't know.

LISA. Am I supposed to fall to my knees?

DON. I don't know.

LISA. Tell me, can't they see how *crude* they are?

DON. Probably not.

LISA. Really? (*Pause.*)

DON. I don't know.

LISA. Well, *I* don't know.

DON. You want another?

LISA. No. Thanks. (*Pause.*)

DON. So what do you do when you're not waiting tables?

LISA. How do you mean?

DON. I mean that's not all you do.

LISA. Yes it is.

DON. Well, what do you *wanna* do . . .

LISA. When I grow up?

DON. Yeah.

LISA. I am grown up. This is as big as I get. (*Pause.*) I don't know, I'm taking some classes.

DON. You are.

LISA. Over at the Art Students' League.

DON. Well.

LISA. Sculpture.

DON. You must be really talented.

LISA. Actually I'm not. (*Pause.*) Not talented enough.

DON. Maybe I could see your work.

LISA. Maybe you could.

DON. I love sculpture.

LISA. Huh.

DON. It's very rich, very sensuous. Humanistically speaking.

LISA. Don.

DON. Yeah?

LISA. Don't try so hard, okay? (*Pause.*)

DON. How about another drink?

LISA. No.

DON. Come on.

LISA. No, it's okay.

DON. *One* more . . .

LISA. Are you trying to get me drunk?

DON. Of course.

LISA. And then what happens?

DON. We go back to my place and I show you my flak jacket. (*Pause.*)

LISA. I know that was supposed to be endearing.

DON. I was only making a joke.

LISA. Who gave you the idea that was funny? (*Pause.*)

DON. I don't seem to be able to say the right thing to you.

LISA. I'm sorry.

DON. I mean, you were talking before—

LISA. I know. I'm . . . thanks for asking me out. I had a good time. Really.

DON. If you think I'm trying to offend you—

LISA. Yes, yes, it's all right. Shall we go? (*Pause. Lisa reaches for the check. Don grabs it at the same time. They hold it between them.*) Please, Don, let me pay for this.

DON. No, I've got it.

LISA. I'd like to. You paid for the film.

DON. This is more.

LISA. Don't be silly.

DON. It's covered.

LISA. Don, please.

DON. I've got plenty of money, okay? You're my date, I'm paying for the fucking check! All right? (*Pause.*) I'm sorry,

Lisa. I'm very sorry. You, ah . . . you . . . I can't figure you out.

LISA. I'm not that complicated.

DON. We're not really hitting it off, are we?

LISA. We don't appear to be.

DON. I do like sculpture.

LISA. Yes.

DON. I don't know much about it. (*Pause.*) I don't know what I'm saying. (*Pause.*)

LISA. Do you enjoy being a man?

DON. It's okay. (*Pause.*) Do you enjoy being a woman?

LISA. Not really. (*Pause.*)

DON. Would you like to come home with me?

LISA. Only if you let me pay the check. (*Pause. He hands her the check. Blackout.*)

Scene 5

Don's room. Don sits on the bed in his underwear, struggling to stay awake. Phil is asleep in a chair, head hanging back. Jack stands over him, watching.

JACK. Don. (*Louder.*) Don. Come here.

DON. What is it?

JACK. You gotta see this. Come here. Come *on.* (*Don gets up.*) Quiet, quiet . . . (*Don joins Jack.*) Look at him. (*Don looks at Phil.*)

DON. So?

JACK. Look at his eyes. (*Don looks at Phil more closely. Pause.*)

DON. Oh man.

JACK. What did I tell you?

DON. That is *weird.* His *eyes* are open.

JACK. It was all the talk of Boys' Bunk Twelve.

DON. You sure he can't see us? (*Jack wriggles his fingers in front of Phil's face.*) How can he sleep like that? I mean . . .

JACK. I know. It's a very disturbing concept.

DON. Yeah, it sure is. (*Pause. Don yawns. Jack lights up a joint.*)

JACK. So, Don, you vicious party beast, what's up next in

our parade of pleasure?
DON. I don't know.
JACK. Twisted sex? Substance abuse? Senseless acts of violence?
DON. Maybe we should pack it in.
JACK. *What?*
DON. Well . . .
JACK. You didn't *mean* that.
DON. That's right, I didn't.
JACK. No, what we're going to *do* is, we're going to have a contest.
DON. Why not.
JACK. I want you to reach back, Don, deep into that ravaged brain of yours, I want you to think hard and tell me . . . three things that happened in the nineteen-seventies. (*Pause.*)
DON. We already did that, Jack.
JACK. We did?
DON. We did that one like a month ago.
JACK. Oh. (*Pause.*) Did we enjoy it?
PHIL. (*In his sleep.*) Mom, I'm home.
DON. What?
JACK. Oh, this is great, he's talking in his sleep.
DON. Makes two of us.
JACK. Phil's really a fascinating guy when he's unconscious. Living next door to him expanded my horizons. (*In Phil's ear.*) Philip, this is your mother.
PHIL. Mom . . .
JACK. I have something to tell you. You're not really our son. You're adopted.
DON. Hey, don't do that.
JACK. We found you in the hold of a Lebanese freighter . . .
DON. Jack, leave him alone.
JACK. Gosh, Mrs. Cleaver, Theodore and I were only playing.
DON. You might be doing something to him.
JACK. Not Phil. He's got an iron constitution.
DON. You treat him like that when you guys were growing up?

23

JACK. Yes, as a matter of fact.

DON. You ever think he might not like it?

JACK. I always assumed he'd be grateful for the attention. I know I would be. (*Pause.*) Anything on the tube?

DON. There's a guide thing under the clothes there.

JACK. You expect me to touch those?

DON. It's clean, I just haven't folded it yet. Hey, come on, don't start throwing everything around. It's not in the books—

JACK. (*Picking up a paperback.*) *Clans of the Alphane Moon.* Spaceships, how can you read this stuff?

DON. I like it.

JACK. (*Reading off the back.*) "A planet of madmen was the key to Earth's survival!"

DON. (*Reaching for it.*) Come on, Jack, put it down.

JACK. (*Opening a page at random.*) "His efforts to make a sensible equation out of the situation—"

DON. Jack come on—

JACK. "—out of the situation—"

DON. Jack—

JACK. "—the situation had borne fruit—"

DON. You're *bending* the *cover*! (*Pause.*)

JACK. (*Dropping the book.*) Nothing personal, Don, but you're one of the most anal slobs I know.

DON. Thank you.

JACK. I mean, it was fine when we lived like this in *college* . . . (*He finds the listings.*) Here we are. Let's see, we got, hmm, "Famine '88" . . . "World at War" . . . whoa, tits and car crashes on HBO!

DON. I don't get cable.

JACK. *What?* Are you serious?

DON. I'm not paying to watch TV.

JACK. You gotta get cable, Don. You're showing your age around here.

DON. *Okay,* boss.

PHIL. (*In his sleep.*) It's like your tongue. (*They both look at Phil. He rolls over. The alarm clock rings. Don shuts it off. Pause.*)

DON. Time to get up.

JACK. Working the night shift?

DON. Guess I set it wrong.

24

JACK. Don, let me ask you a question.
DON. Uhm.
JACK. Every time I come here, you're always in your under-wear.
DON. So?
JACK. Don't you own any pants?
DON. I like to be prepared.
JACK. For what?
DON. Going to sleep.
JACK. Are we hinting at something?
DON. Forget it.
JACK. Hey, if you want me to go don't just sit there in your shorts in*sinu*ating. Just tell me. Look me in the eye and say, Listen here Jack, I'm sorry, it's late, I can *see* you've got *things* on your *mind* but I'd rather go to sleep than sit here in my ratty underwear listening to you. Be honest, Don. Don't get all *ironic* for fuck's sake. Keep me away from irony.
DON. Now listen here, Jack . . .
JACK. Yes?
DON. Have another beer. (*He hands Jack a beer.*)
JACK. Thank you. (*He opens it but does not drink. Pause.*)
DON. So what's on your mind?
JACK. Did I say something was on my mind?
DON. You hinted at it ironically.
JACK. Don, if you knew anything about me at all, you'd know this: Nothing ever bothers me.
DON. You're lucky that way.
JACK. Luck's got nothing to do with it. It's a matter of style. Image. You have a problem, just ask yourself one simple question: What would Ray Charles do in a situation like this? And Ray, I think, hipster that he is—
DON. What problem?
JACK. *The* problem, whatever problem you're *talking* about, I don't know. But Ray, Badass *Ray*—
PHIL. I don't know, is this my house?
JACK. Fucking myna bird in a sport coat here.
DON. What problems.
JACK. You heard the latest? This girl, he's been seeing her a week, every night he goes to her place, right, they talk

25

about the whales or something, he gets to sleep on the couch. She says she's frigid. He says it doesn't matter. She says her uncle raped her when she was ten. He says I love you. She says maybe you shouldn't come by anymore. He says let's give it time. She says I'm screwing somebody else. He says it's all right, we can work around it. Isn't that so *typical*?

DON. Poor guy.

JACK. Calls me up, he says Jack, listen, I'm scared to be alone tonight—

DON. When?

JACK. This, tonight. What am I gonna do, say no? I mean, a friend's a friend. No matter how you look at it. (*Pause. Lowering his voice.*) But I'll tell you something about Phil.

DON. Yeah?

JACK. He's a homo.

DON. What?

JACK. Gay as a coot.

DON. Are you kidding? He told you?

JACK. No he didn't *tell* me, he doesn't even know it.

DON. How do you know it?

JACK. Don, look at the women he goes out with. They eat Kal Kan for breakfast. And *they* all dump *him*. That's not normal.

DON. Is this for real?

JACK. Look at the facts. (*Pause.*)

DON. Well . . . so?

JACK. *So?*

DON. So he's, you know, so what? (*Pause.*)

JACK. Exactly, so what?

DON. I mean in this day and age . . .

JACK. At this point in time, yes, Don, I know what you're saying, you're right, absolutely right. Absolutely.

DON. So what are we *arguing*?

JACK. We're not arguing, we're discussing.

DON. What are we discussing?

JACK. We're not discussing anything. (*Pause.*)

DON. Won't your wife be worried?

JACK. About what?

DON. Where you are.

26

JACK. Nah. Actually . . . actually she's out of town right now.
DON. Is she?
JACK. Her bank sent her out there, out to, ah, Ohio. Gonna finance another goddamn shopping mall.
DON. She must be doing pretty well, they trust her with that.
JACK. Somebody's gotta put bread on the table.
DON. You guys have a great arrangement.
JACK. I thank Jesus every day. (*Pause.*)
DON. So who's taking care of Jason?
JACK. Well, he's out there with her.
DON. Out there in Ohio.
JACK. It's the kind of place you want to see when you're young.
DON. Sure.
JACK. They'll be back pretty soon.
DON. Yeah. (*Pause.*)
JACK. How's your sex life, Don?
DON. Well, you know.
JACK. I don't know, that's why I'm asking.
DON. It's fine, I'm seeing this girl.
JACK. Well well.
DON. Yeah.
JACK. Well well *well*. What's she like?
DON. She's ah . . . she's sort of . . . I guess she's kind of serious. You know? Very . . . thoughtful. We talk a lot.
JACK. I bet.
DON. No, it's . . . she's always asking me questions. Why do I do this, do I say that . . . we talk about how we feel, about things, and . . . I'm learning to be responsible . . . and, ah . . .
JACK. Tits?
DON. They're okay.
JACK. Hmm. Well, I wish you luck. (*Pause.*)
DON. Actually she may be coming over a little later.
JACK. A *little* later? It's fucking three in the morning.
DON. She's a waitress over by the park, finishes at four.
JACK. Sounds pretty devoted.
DON. Well.

27

JACK. So why you been keeping her a secret?
DON. She's not a secret, she's . . . you know . . .
JACK. A waitress.
DON. She's really a sculptor.
JACK. Does she get paid for that?
DON. Not yet, no.
JACK. Is she in a *museum*?
DON. She just started . . .
JACK. So she's a dabbler, right? She's a waitress who dabbles, nothing to be ashamed of. Why don't you say that, does it embarrass you?
DON. No . . .
JACK. Really? (*He rubs his face. Phil mutters in his sleep.*) Hey, you wanna go bowling? That's right, you can't.
DON. What did you mean by that?
JACK. Bowling. Duck pins. Sport of Kings.
DON. About being a waitress.
JACK. Huh? I don't know, that's what she is, right? I didn't mean anything. You wanna go?
DON. It was insulting, Jack.
JACK. I didn't mean it to be.
DON. No, okay, you didn't, but it was. You do that all the time.
JACK. What's this about?
DON. Listen, you could be a little more considerate, all right?
JACK. What am I, your therapist?
DON. Jesus, you're doing it again!
JACK. What?
DON. You're insulting me!
JACK. Oh come on, don't be an asshole.
DON. *Stop* it!
JACK. I'm not doing anything, Don. Why are you getting so excited? Are you under orders? This is not like you. She's a waitress, she's a sculptress, fuck do I care I never even *met* her, tell me—
DON. I feel you really—
JACK. You *feel*, everybody *feels*, *fuck* that. What are you, are you a man? Can't you control yourself? You're *opening up*. You're being *sensitive*. That's a nice *trick*, Don. But don't let

28

it go to your head or you'll wind up getting yanked around by the wiener. (*Pause.*) As they say in the vernacular.

DON. I am not getting "yanked around."

JACK. I didn't say you were, I merely—

DON. Then take it back.

JACK. Okay, I hit a sore spot—

DON. Take it back.

JACK. Please, don't *be* this way—

DON. Take it back! (*Pause.*)

JACK. All right, Don. Shhh. All right. This is childish. Be cool. Be *cool.* It's me, remember? Not some lady you're trying to bring home. We *know* each other. We know what we really are. We're men, Don. We do terrible things. Let's admit we like them and start from there. You want to be a different person? Get a hug, all the bad thoughts disappear? I'm sorry, it won't *work* that way. It's not like changing your shirt, we can't *promise* to be better. That's a lie. What do you want, Don? Be honest. Do what you *want.* Please. I beg you. Because if you don't, what kind of ma . . . what are you gonna be then? (*Don says nothing.*) I am your friend, Don. I care about you. I really do. Okay? (*Don says nothing.*) So you wanna go bowling? Hey, I got some amyl, you wanna do amyl? Don?

PHIL. All my shoes . . . line 'em up . . .

JACK. (*To Don.*) What you want, Don. Just think about it. (*Pause.*)

DON. Yeah.

JACK. (*Poking Phil.*) Phil, wake up, we gotta go. (*Phil rolls over. Jack looks at him. To Don.*) Hey, you wanna see something? You'll get a kick out of this, it's up your alley. (*He hands Don a piece of notepaper with crayon markings on it.*) Jason left that. Go ahead, read it aloud.

DON. "Dear Daddy, Mommy is taking me on jet. We are going to planet light blue. It has a river, and some caves called feeling caves, a waterfall, beds, and slides. There is a city there called 'girls are for you.' I know that is true. I love you but I think I am going to stay here." (*Pause.*) Sounds better than Ohio.

JACK. Yeah right. (*Pause.*) You know, I read that and I thought . . . what the fuck does this mean? Is he insane?

What is going on inside this kid's head? I watch him, right, he's this tiny guy, really, his sneakers are like this big . . . but something's going on in there. Something's going on. (*Pause.*) When he was born, did I tell you this? . . . He—

DON. (*Handing back the note.*) She's an artist, Jack. Not a waitress. Understand? (*Pause.*)

JACK. Yes, Don. Of course. Thank you. I'm glad we could have this little moment together. Only listen, Don . . . (*Pause.*) Don't forget who your friends are. (*He leans into Phil's ear.*) Phil.

PHIL. Huh?

JACK. Time to go home.

PHIL. Go?

JACK. Come on.

PHIL. Fell asleep.

JACK. No kidding. (*A knock on the door.*)

DON. (*Getting up.*) Oh Jesus.

PHIL. Feel rotten. (*Don meets Lisa at the door and blocks her entrance.*)

LISA. Hi.

DON. You're early.

LISA. You're right. Nice legs.

PHIL. I'm never looking at another woman again.

JACK. Very practical.

LISA. What's going on?

DON. Some friends came by.

PHIL. I've done bad things, Jack. So many bad things.

LISA. Sorry to disturb you.

DON. Don't start.

LISA. I only ran over here in the middle of the night.

JACK. (*Singing.*) "Well, I used to be disgusted . . ."

LISA. Are you going to introduce us?

DON. Guys, this is Lisa. Lisa, this is Jack. That's Phil. He sleeps with his eyes open.

JACK. Young Theodore is afraid of the dark.

LISA. Excuse me?

JACK. I said he's afraid of the dark.

LISA. I thought his name was Phil.

JACK. I was making a joke.

LISA. Why?

JACK. In order to be funny.

LISA. Well. So you're the funny one.

JACK. Have we met before?

LISA. No. But we know who we are.

DON. You want me to call you a cab? Jack? (*Jack walks up to Lisa. He puts his arm around Don. He smiles.*)

JACK. Don tells me you're a very talented sculptress. (*Blackout.*)

SCENE 6

The park. Jack and Phil sitting on a bench. Jack with a child's toy in his hand. Phil looking out front.

PHIL. I would have destroyed myself for this woman. Gladly. I would have eaten garbage. I would have sliced my *wrists* open. Under the right circumstances, I mean, if she said, "Hey, Phil, why don't you just cut your wrists open," well, come on, but if *seriously* . . . We clicked, we connected on so many things, right off the bat, we talked about God for *three hours* once, I don't know what good it did, but that *intensity* . . . and the first time we went to bed, I didn't even touch her. I didn't *want* to, understand what I'm saying? And you know, I played it very casually, because, all right, I've had some rough experiences, I'm the first to admit, but after a couple of weeks I could feel we were right there, so I laid it down, everything I wanted to tell her, and . . . and she says to me . . . she says . . . "Nobody should ever need another person that badly." Do you *believe* that? "Nobody should ever . . ."! What is that? Is that something you saw on TV? I dump my *heart* on the table, you give me Joyce Dr. Fucking Brothers? "Need, need," I'm saying I *love* you, is that wrong? Is that not allowed anymore? (*Pause. Jack looks at him.*) And so what if I did need her? Is that so bad? All right, crucify me, I needed her! So *what*! I don't want to be by myself, I'm by myself I feel like I'm going out of my mind, I do. I sit there, I'm thinking forget it, I'm not gonna make it through the next *ten seconds*, I just can't *stand* it. But I do, somehow, I get through the ten seconds, but then I have to do it all over again, cause they just keep coming, all these . . . seconds, floating by, while I'm waiting for something to happen, I don't know what, a car wreck, a nuclear war or something, that sounds awful but at least there'd be this *instant* when I'd know I was alive. Just once. Cause I look in the mirror, and I can't believe I'm really there. I can't believe that's me. It's like my body, right, is the size of, what, the Statue of Liberty, and I'm inside it, I'm down in one of the legs, this gigantic hairy leg, I'm scraping around inside my own foot like some tiny fetus. And I don't know who I am, or where I'm going. And I wish I'd never been born. (*Pause.*) Not only that, my hair is falling out, and that really *sucks.* (*Pause.*)

JACK. You know, Phil, in Cambodia . . . they don't have *time* to worry about things like that.

PHIL. Maybe I'll move there.

JACK. Well, keep in touch.

PHIL. Or maybe I'll just kill myself.

JACK. Hmm. (*Pause.*) Hey, Phil.

PHIL. What.

JACK. Let's see that smile.

PHIL. Leave me alone.

JACK. Ah, come on.

PHIL. Get *away.*

JACK. Come on, Phil, I see it, I see that smile, come on, come *on,* ooo, here it comes—

PHIL. I'm not *gonna.*

JACK. Yes you are, come on, just a little, just a weensy, just an unsey bunsey, just a meensee neensee, just a—

PHIL. All right, God damn it! I'm smiling, okay? I'm happy, oh I'm so *happy,* ha ha ha! I hate when you do this.

JACK. One day you'll miss me, Phil.

PHIL. Probably. (*Pause. He looks out.*) Well, Jason seems to be enjoying himself.

JACK. Why wouldn't he be?

PHIL. I don't know. He just seems . . . glad to be back.

JACK. I don't see what you're getting at.

PHIL. I'm just saying it's . . . good that . . . you and Carla . . . worked it out.

JACK. Worked what out?

PHIL. Whatever it was. Between you.

JACK. There was nothing "between" us, Phil.

PHIL. Oh. Okay.

JACK. If there *was* something "between" us, we'd sit down and discuss it like reasonable adults. We'd come to an agreement. We'd draw up certain rules, and then we'd follow them. Our feelings don't have to enter *into* it. (*Pause.*)

PHIL. Well, she's a lovely girl, Jack.

JACK. She is, Phil. She certainly is. And I'm the luckiest palooka. (*Pause.*) So . . . you heard from Don lately?

PHIL. No. What's he up to?

JACK. That's what I'm asking you.

PHIL. I don't know, he doesn't call me. Why would he call me?

JACK. He might be trying to get in touch with me.

PHIL. Why wouldn't he just call *you*?

JACK. Well, maybe he *has*, but I've been busy, Phil. I don't have time to sit around staring at the phone. I have *things* to *do*. I have food to eat and records to play. I've got places I have to be at and then come back from. I've got miles to go before I sleep. *All* sorts of stuff. (*Pause.*) Darn it, who needs him? Let him play with his dolls. We're having a heck of a time all by ourselves, aren't we little fella?

PHIL. I guess.

JACK. Ho, you bet we *are*. (*Pause.*) You *bet* we are. (*Pause.*) You know, Phil, what was the biggest mistake we ever made in our lives?

PHIL. What? (*Maggie enters, in running gear. Jack sees her. Pause.*)

JACK. (*To Phil.*) What?

PHIL. You were gonna say—

JACK. Was I? (*To Maggie.*) That's our face!

MAGGIE. (*Seeing him.*) Well, hello.

JACK. Miss, I've never seen you before, but how would you like to be a star?

PHIL. Jack . . .

MAGGIE. Might be fun.

JACK. *Fun?* My friend here is too shy to mention it, but he happens to be the associate producer of a new major mo-

33

tion picture. And frankly you've just saved him a trip across the continent. (*To Phil.*) Go ahead, tell her about the picture.

PHIL. I, ah . . . um . . .

JACK. The picture is a modern picture. It's an American picture. It's the modern story of American men and their modern American women, set against a backdrop as modern and American as all indoors. It's a spectacle, it's an epic, it's the story of a generation that had it all and couldn't figure out what to do with it. And it's the story of a girl, one special girl, and her quest for meaning in a world she never made. And of the man who wouldn't rest until he tracked her down.

MAGGIE. Why would he do that?

JACK. He couldn't think of anything better to do.

MAGGIE. Sounds stupid.

JACK. That's why I say. I keep telling him to make a teenage sex farce, but does he listen? (*To Phil.*) Do you listen?

PHIL. What?

JACK. He never listens!

MAGGIE. How's your ward?

JACK. Discreet as ever.

MAGGIE. Good to know.

JACK. How's life at the waxworks?

MAGGIE. Don't ask me.

JACK. Believe me, I won't. (*Pause.*)

MAGGIE. Mind if I sit?

JACK. Mind if she sits?

PHIL. No . . . I—

JACK. We don't mind if you sit. (*Maggie sits between Jack and Phil. Pause.*)

PHIL. My name's Phil, by the way.

MAGGIE. Hello, Phil.

PHIL. This is my friend Jack.

MAGGIE. (*Laughing.*) Hello, Jack. (*Jack nods.*)

PHIL. You two know each other?

MAGGIE. Do we know each other?

JACK. We don't know each other.

PHIL. Oh.

MAGGIE. Ever feel you're about to do something you're really going to regret?
JACK. Never. (*Pause.*)
PHIL. Well, hey . . . so you been out doing some *running,* huh? (*Maggie and Jack look at each other. They smile. Blackout.*)

SCENE 7

Lights up. Don and a girl in bed. Night. A lit candle sits in a saucer.

GIRL. Something is coming to get me. I've never seen it, but I know it's there. It thinks about me all the time. One night I'll wake up for no reason and it will be with me. And in that moment I will realize that this is my last minute on Earth. (*Pause.*) Are you still up?
DON. Yeah.
GIRL. I have visions. I close my eyes and see things. There's nothing I can do about it. Once I closed my eyes and I saw a plane going down in a jungle. Inside a boy and girl were sucking on an orange. Their bodies were eaten by monkeys. Another time I saw an old man sitting on a porch. He had just put pomade in his hair. He said, Mike, clean that blade and stick it in the garage. I have no idea what that was about at all.
DON. You saw this?
GIRL. I didn't *see* it, but I *saw* it, you know? (*Pause.*)
DON. Do you like working in the record store?
GIRL. I don't work in a record store.
DON. I bought a record from you.
GIRL. I was only pretending to work there. I do that sometimes, go into a place and pretend I work there.
DON. Why?
GIRL. I'm mentally ill.
DON. Oh.
GIRL. Does that disturb you?
DON. It depends.
GIRL. On what?
DON. Whether it's true or not.

GIRL. I used to be a lot worse. When I was fourteen I weighed eighty pounds. I didn't eat. I was trying to make myself disappear. Getting rid of my flesh seemed easy. But I couldn't figure out how to get rid of my bones. That's the hardest part.

DON. I imagine it would be.

GIRL. You don't believe me, do you?

DON. I didn't say that.

GIRL. What would you think if I told you my father tried to run me over with a steamroller?

DON. Hmm . . . well . . .

GIRL. He was a daredevil. There were six capes in his closet. I was part of the act. He would tie me up and put me in a laundry bag. Then he would come at me in a steamroller. I had thirty seconds to escape. What you have to do is totally relax your muscles. Then the cords slip right off. But my father would tie double knots.

DON. Why?

GIRL. He wanted to kill me.

DON. Why did he want to do that?

GIRL. Because he wasn't allowed to fuck me. *(Silence. Don looks uncomfortable. Suddenly he gets out of bed and reaches for his shirt.)* What's wrong?

DON. Nothing. Excuse me.

GIRL. Where are you going?

DON. Out. Don't worry. I just have to go. Uh, listen, the front door locks itself so just slam it on your way out.

GIRL. I don't understand, you're leaving?

DON. I think I . . . um, there's some Hi-C in the fridge, help yourself, okay, and I'll, we'll talk later . . .

GIRL. Have I upset you?

DON. No, no . . .

GIRL. Was it something I said?

DON. Look, I'm sorry, it was nice meeting you, but I don't think . . . you and I should . . .

GIRL. Don't you like me?

DON. It's not a question of that—

GIRL. What did I do wrong?

DON. Nothing. Really.

GIRL. Please, ah . . . please, come here. I know I'm

strange. I can't help it . . . Listen, I can tell fortunes. Did you know that? I can. Would you let me tell your fortune?

DON. What?

GIRL. Give me your hand. Please? I know this is upsetting you. I can't help it. Just give me your hand. Then you can go. (*Pause.*) Please? (*Pause. Don gives her his hand.*) There, yes. That's better. This is very good. Now . . . calm yourself. Clear your mind. Yes . . . yes. Are you relaxed? Nod your head. (*Don nods his head.*) Ah, yes. This is the hand of a man. Very strong. Very powerful. This is a hand that will perform great acts. Terrible, but great. It will hurt many people. But it will seldom be raised in anger. It is the hand of a compassionate man. A man with a large soul. (*Pause.*) Should I go on?

DON. Okay.

GIRL. You feel that you have yet to live. That the years are passing like a dream. This is true. But soon all that will change. People will flock to you. Men . . .

DON. Women?

GIRL. Women, yes. They will be drawn to you. To your power. It cannot be hidden. (*Pause.*)

DON. How will I die?

GIRL. At sea. When you are very old. Your body will never be found. (*Pause.*)

DON. You're scaring the shit out of me.

GIRL. Everything will be all right.

DON. Do you work in the record store or not?

GIRL. It doesn't matter. Come here.

DON. I'm not going to able to see you again . . .

GIRL. Yes.

DON. I shouldn't be doing this . . . I'm gonna get in trouble . . .

GIRL. A man can do anything he wants. I'm blowing out the candle now. Are you going to stay?

Don. Well . . .

GIRL. Then come to bed. (*Don gets into bed. Pause.*)

DON. Are any of the things you told me true?

GIRL. They're true if you think they're true. (*Pause.*)

DON. Do *you* think they're true? (*The girl looks at DON. Pause. She blows out the candle. Blackout.*)

SCENE 8

Lights up on Don's room. Lisa stands, Don sits on the edge of the bed. They are both in their underwear. Lisa holds a pair of panties. Silence.)

LISA. And that's all you have to say about it?

DON. What else do you want me to say?

LISA. How about sorry?

DON. Well, of course I'm sorry. How could I not be sorry?

LISA. You haven't *said* it.

DON. I'm sorry.

LISA. No you're not. (*Pause.*) I'm going. (*She starts gathering her clothes.*)

DON. Um—

LISA. What?

DON. I, ah—

LISA. YES? WHAT? WHAT IS IT?

DON. I just think you should realize that I've been under a lot of strain lately.

LISA. I see.

DON. And maybe, I've, you know, handled some things badly—

LISA. You're under a lot of strain so you go off and fuck somebody else.

DON. That's unnecessarily blunt.

LISA. Christ but you're a cheeky bastard. Couldn't you even bother to clean up before I came? Put away the odd pair of panties?

DON. I thought they were yours.

LISA. I don't buy my panties at *Job* Lot, Don. And I have a low opinion of people who do. (*She throws the panties at him. He fools with them and puts them over his head like a cap.*)

DON. They keep your ears warm.

LISA. You think I'm kidding, don't you? You think, well, Lisa's just having a little *episode*, it'll all blow over, chalk it up to boyish exuberance, hit the sack? Who the fuck do you think you are, James Bond? (*Pause.*) Did you use a condom?

DON. Huh?

LISA. A *condom*. You know what they are. You see them on TV all the time.

DON. Wha—why?

LISA. Because you slept with her, and then you slept with me, and you don't know who she's been fucking, do you, *Don*. DO YOU. (*Pause.*) I'm going.

DON. Where?

LISA. I'm going to lie down in traffic, Don. I'm going to let a crosstown bus roll over me because my life is meaningless since you betrayed me. I'm going to my *apartment*, you stupid shithead!

DON. Lisa, it was just a very casual thing. It's over.

LISA. What do I care?

DON. I made a mistake, I admit that, but . . .

LISA. But what?

DON. It made me realize something, something very important.

LISA. Yes?

DON. (*Very softly.*) I love you.

LISA. What? I can't hear you.

DON. I said I—

LISA. I *heard* what you said! "You love me"! That doesn't mean shit! This isn't high school, I'm wearing your *pin*. You want me to tell you what really counts? Out here with the graduates?

DON. What?

LISA. It's not worth it! Do what you want, it doesn't matter to me. I don't even know you, Don. After four months I don't know who you are or why you do what you do. You keep getting your dick stuck in things. What is that all about, anyway? Will someone please explain that to me? (*Pause.*) Don't look at me that way.

DON. What way?

LISA. Like a whipped dog. It's just pathetic.

DON. Lisa, please. I did something very stupid. I won't do it again.

LISA. Do you have any idea what you're saying?

DON. I'm saying I feel bad.

LISA. I'm sorry, but "I feel bad" isn't even in the running. Not at all. We're talking about faith. *Semper fidelis*, like the

Marines. They don't leave people lying in foxholes. They just do it. They don't "feel bad."

DON. How do you know so much about the Marines?

LISA. It's not the Marines, Don. It's got nothing to do with the fucking Marines. It's the idea. (*Pause.*) You don't understand what I'm talking about, do you? You're just afraid of being punished. I'm not you're *mother*. I don't spank. (*Pause.*) I'm going. Have fun fucking your bargain shopper and cracking jokes with your creepy friends.

DON. Lisa, wait, I have to tell you something.

LISA. No you don't.

DON. I had this dream about you last night.

LISA. How inconvenient.

DON. Can I tell you this? Just for a minute? Please? (*Pause.*)

LISA. *Start.*

DON. Okay . . . okay . . . now . . . I was . . . flying. In a plane, I mean a rocket. It was a rocket ship. And I was all alone inside. With nothing to eat but junk food in rocks along the walls—sandwich cremes, Raisinets, boxes and boxes of crap. The smell was nauseating.

LISA. Does this go on much longer?

DON. Anyway I looked outside and there was this tiny planet floating by me like a blue Nerf ball. So I opened a bottle of Yoohoo and sat down to relax. But it must have been doped because it knocked me right out. When I woke up . . . the cabin was on fire! I tried to move but someone had tied me to the chair with piano wire, it was slicing into my wrists like they were chunks of ham. The ship was in a nosedive and I was slammed against the seat. Suddenly, bam, the whole port side blew away. I could see the planet rolling beneath me. A new world, Lisa. Pristine, unsullied. Virgin. I reached out . . . and the ship broke up around me in a sheet of flames. I was tied to a chair falling through the void. My mind left me. (*Pause.*) When I came to I was lying on a beach half buried in the sand. My right hand was gone. The wire had severed it at the wrist. Leeches sucked on the stump. I rolled over and waited for death. And then . . . you rose from the water on a bed of seaweed. On the white sands your hips swayed with an animal rhythm. I don't know why you were there. I didn't ask. You knelt down and gave me nectar from a gourd. You healed me in the shade of the trees. And you never spoke. And neither did I. I had forgotten how. Later on we built a shelter. You bore many children while I caught fish with a spear in the blue light of three moons. And then, one day, we lay ourselves down together on the sand. The breath eased from our bodies. And we died. And the ocean ate our bones. (*Pause.*)

LISA. What a crock of shit. You expect me to believe that?

DON. It's true. I dreamt it.

LISA. You've got a vivid imagination, I'll grant you that much. Very. . . . charming. Very romantic.

DON. It's an omen. It's like a prophecy.

LISA. Of what?

DON. Of us. The two of us, together.

LISA. Well. (*Pause.*) You'd probably make me do the fishing.

DON. I wouldn't. I promise. (*Pause.*)

LISA. Wait. Wait. This is not it. This is nothing. I can't even talk to you until you tell me the truth. Why did you do this, Don? When you knew I trusted you? Was it her breasts, her buttocks, the smell of her sweat? Was it her underwear? Was it because she wasn't me? Did you have a reason? Any reason at all?

DON. I wanted to see . . . if I could get away with it.

LISA. Why?

DON. Because that's what a man would do. (*Pause.*) Let's get married, Lisa. I want to marry you. I want to be faithful to you forever. I want to put my head on your lap. Can I do that? I want to bury my face in your lap. I don't want to think about anything. Is that okay? (*Pause.*)

LISA. Would you like to play a little game, Don?

DON. What kind of game?

LISA. A pretend game. Let's pretend you could do anything you wanted to. And whatever you did, nobody could blame you for it. Not me or anyone else. You would be totally free. You wouldn't have to make promises and you wouldn't have to lie. All you would have to do is know how you feel. Just that. How would that be?

41

DON. I don't know.
LISA. Just pretend. What would you do? (*Pause.*)
DON. I think I would be . . . different?
LISA. Would you?
DON. I'd like to be.
LISA. Different how? (*Pause.*)
DON. Well . . . I would . . . I think I would . . . I think maybe I . . . (*He pauses and falls into a long silence. Blackout.*)

SCENE 9

In the blackout, the bandleader's voice.

BANDLEADER. All right, everybody, before you get *too* comfortable in your chairs, let's see if we can work off a little of that delicious roast beef with some of today's young sounds. (*A small, accordian-led combo strikes up with "Beat It."* Lights up on Phil and Jack seated at a round banquet table littered with napkins, glasses, and half-eaten dinners. Jack has a row of soda-filled glasses lined up in front of him. He methodically pours sugar into them one by one, watching as they foam up explosively. Phil stares straight ahead.*)
PHIL. (*After a while.*) Christ, I hate weddings. They're so depressing, you know? They remind me of funerals.
JACK. Weddings remind you of funerals?
PHIL. They remind me of death.
JACK. Everything reminds you of death, Phil.
PHIL. No it doesn't.
JACK. What are you thinking about right now?
PHIL. Well, I'm thinking about death. But only because you brought it up.
JACK. I didn't bring it up, you brought it up.
PHIL. No I didn't.
JACK. You said you hate weddings because they remind you of death.
PHIL. People are drinking those, you know.
JACK. Not anymore.

*See Special Note on copyright page.

42

PHIL. That is so childish, Jack.

JACK. Is it?

PHIL. You don't think so?

JACK. Well . . . (*He pauses and bursts out laughing.*)

PHIL. Why don't you grow up?

JACK. You need some more dope. You'll feel better.

PHIL. I don't *want* to feel better. I wish I was dead.

JACK. You gotten laid lately, Phil?

PHIL. What do you care?

JACK. I like to know my friends are happy.

PHIL. I think that's incredibly tactless.

JACK. Well, I'm sorry you see it that way. (*Pause.*) So you *haven't* gotten laid?

PHIL. You're so curious, yes, yes, I have *gotten laid*, is that okay?

JACK. Yes, that's fine. (*Pause.*)

PHIL. You don't have any idea what it's like, Jack. You're completely out of it. You've got your wife and your kid. You've got stability. You don't have to make yourself crawl through the gutter to get regular sex. When I think of some of the things I've done . . . it just makes me feel sick. (*Pause.*)

JACK. Like for instance?

PHIL. Oh, please.

JACK. No, I mean what things?

PHIL. I'm not here to provide you with titillation.

JACK. Yes you are, Phil. You just don't know it. (*Pause. Out front.*) There she goes, the old Earth Mother . . . Hi, Honey! No, we're doing fine, we're dandy . . . Look at her, she's plastered across the walls. One drink and she's ready for pearl diving without a loincloth. She won't keep booze in the house, you know. Jason might invite some nursery buddies in for an afternoon mixer. Not to mention she wants the VCR disconnected, she thinks he needs *more creative* playtime so she bought these toys from Scandinavia, and you know what they are, they're unpainted blocks of wood, you're supposed to have fun *arranging* them. You look at these things and you know why the Swedes keep offing themselves. So I tell her—

PHIL. If you must know, I fucked a girl while she was

unconscious.
JACK. Beg pardon?
PHIL. You want to know so I'm telling you!
JACK. You . . . fucked a girl while she was . . . unconscious?
PHIL. Yes.
JACK. How?
PHIL. I deserve to die.
JACK. I'll decide that, Phil. Just what have you done?
PHIL. I didn't *do* anything. She blinked off.
JACK. When? Where?
PHIL. We went out, we came back to her place—
JACK. Who is this?
PHIL. You don't know her.
JACK. What does she look like?
PHIL. You don't *know* her.
JACK. Did she have nice tits? Just tell me about the tits.
PHIL. It doesn't *matter*.
JACK. Just tell me!
PHIL. They were okay.
JACK. Only okay?
PHIL. No, they were fine.
JACK. Good. Go on.
PHIL. So we came back to her place, one of these sub-divided closets, right, and the radiators are howling. It was like a pizza oven in there. She pours a couple of Scotches, we talk a little. Pretty soon I can tell I won't be coming home tonight.
JACK. You bounder.
PHIL. So I get her blouse off—
JACK. Wait, wait, how'd that happen?
PHIL. Just, you know, in the course of conversation. It's time to make my move, I take her in my arms . . .
JACK. Uh-huh . . .
PHIL. She keels right over. Wham. Right down on the futon.
JACK. Geez.
PHIL. I'm telling you it was *hot* in there.
JACK. I guess so.
PHIL. Anyway, I tried to bring her around, but she'd had a lot to drink, you should have seen the liquor tab, luckily I

44

was able to charge it—so, I thought, isn't this great, this is just the way I wanted to spend my evening. I was pretty pissed off.

JACK. So you fucked her anyway, huh?

PHIL. No! What do you think I am? . . . I decided to put her to bed. I'd sleep on the floor and keep an eye on her. So I did that, but she was sweating so much, it looked un*heal-thy*, so I, ah . . .

JACK. You undressed her, right?

PHIL. I took her shoes off, that's all! I took off her shoes, and she had on these tights, so I thought I better take those off too . . .

JACK. And then you fucked her.

PHIL. I had her undressed and I thought, what the hell, I don't want to sleep on the floor, so I got into bed with her, and. . . . I don't know. I don't know. I walked home afterwards, sixteen blocks at three in the morning. I was hoping somebody would kill me. I felt like . . . you know what's really terrifying? Everyone's worried about the world getting blown up or something, right, but . . . what if it doesn't? What if it just goes on like this, forever? What are we gonna do then? (*Pause.*)

JACK. You sly old dog.

PHIL. What?

JACK. What an operator, huh? You old dog.

PHIL. I feel *awful*.

JACK. Ah, come on, Phil, drop the Hamlet routine. Did you speak to her yet?

PHIL. Yeah. She called me. She said she was sorry she fell asleep and maybe we could go out again.

JACK. And nothing about . . .

PHIL. No.

JACK. So? Everything's fine. You had a little fun, you covered your ass, and no one's the wiser. What's the problem? (*Pause.*)

BANDLEADER. (*Offstage.*) Don and Lisa, we wish you the very best of luck, life, and happiness This song is just for you. (*The combo plays "When I'm Sixty-four."*)*

*See Special Note on copyright page.

PHIL. What did you get them?

JACK. A blender. We had it lying around.

PHIL. I wish I'd thought of that. I bought them a cheese wheel.

JACK. A what?

PHIL. A cheese wheel. A wheel of cheese. It comes in the mail.

JACK. Uh-huh.

PHIL. It's Yarlsberg. Most people like Yarlsberg, don't they?

JACK. I couldn't say, Phil. I know a lot but I don't know that.

PHIL. What the hell, it's not like I see him every day. You catch the bride?

JACK. Yeah, she's a real bowzer, huh?

PHIL. Jack . . .

JACK. What?

PHIL. That's so rude.

JACK. Would you say that girl is attractive?

PHIL. Your attitude towards women—

JACK. Hey, I don't have an *attitude* towards women. I'm not questioning her right to exist. I'm simply asking if you find her attractive.

PHIL. No, I don't.

JACK. So why are you getting upset?

PHIL. Maybe he loves her, did that ever occur to you?

JACK. Of course it *occurred* to me. I'm not an idiot. But that's not going to make her any better looking, is it? So don't give me this attitude bullshit, Phil. I'm just telling the truth. Nobody's going to punish you for telling the truth. (*Silence. Jack moves to pour sugar in Phil's drink.*)

PHIL. Don't do that.

JACK. I'm just *kidding.* (*Pause.*) Hey, you're still working at that place, aren't you?

PHIL. Unfortunately.

JACK. Nine to five?

PHIL. Uh-huh.

JACK. I want you to do me a favor.

PHIL. Like what?

JACK. Like letting me use your apartment during the

daytime.

PHIL. Oh. Well, sure. Why not. (*Pause.*) How come?

JACK. Because I need to be able to be alone in the afternoons.

PHIL. What's wrong with your apartment?

JACK. It's no good.

PHIL. Why's that?

JACK. Why do you think?

PHIL. I don't know.

JACK. You don't have to know, you just have to do me a favor.

PHIL. It's my apartment, Jack. I'd like to know what it's being used for.

JACK. All right, don't do it. Jesus.

PHIL. I mean I trust you, but—

JACK. Are you my friend?

PHIL. Sure.

JACK. Then I need your help. I've got to meet somebody and I can't do it at my place.

PHIL. A woman.

JACK. Yes. She is a woman.

PHIL. I see.

JACK. You'll appreciate the difficulty.

PHIL. Right.

JACK. So you'll do it?

PHIL. Um . . .

JACK. Don't "um," Phil, come on. I'd do it for you.

PHIL. That's a little different, isn't it? I mean . . . I'm single. I'm supposed to do things like that. You're talking about adultery.

JACK. Oh, please.

PHIL. You and another woman, I don't know—

JACK. Let's not get melodramatic. This has nothing to do with adultery. This is just a nice little affair I'm going to let myself have. A quick tour of foreign panties and then it's back on the bus home. Everybody's happy and no one gets hurt. What could be simpler?

PHIL. I don't think I can do it, Jack. I'd just feel too guilty. I'd be helping you to ruin your life.

JACK. You're joking, right?

47

PHIL. Did you tell this girl you're married?
JACK. I've implied as such.
PHIL. But you haven't told her.
JACK. Why am I having this discussion?
PHIL. You're so big on the truth, why didn't you tell her?
JACK. Well, we're up on our little throne, are we? You and your fucking sexual sob stories, you think you know the answer?
PHIL. Yes, I do.
JACK. No you don't. Absolutely not. You want to know the *truth*, you want to know what I have *found out* while you sit there twisting your guilt-ridden nuts off? *It doesn't matter*! It doesn't *matter* what you do because nobody is watching, Phil! Nobody's taking notes, nobody is heating up a pitchfork, there *is* nobody there! So don't dare tell me that I'm doing something wrong, because I decide that, and I decide there *is* nothing wrong. I'm going to commit adultery, Phil! I'm actually going against the Ten Commandments, and as long as I'm careful and don't get caught I don't give a shit.(*Pause.*) Nothing's happening, Phil. Where's the lightning? (*Don enters in a tuxedo.*)
DON. We can't go on meeting like this.
JACK. Hey, here he is, the man of the minute.
DON. You two look like a couple of derelicts. How you doing, Philly?
PHIL. Okay, I'm great.
JACK. Put 'er there, Don. Big Don. Old Big Don.
DON. Why am I Big Don?
JACK. Because you are, that's why. You look like a waiter. Here you go. (*He hands Don a gargantuan joint.*)
DON. Is this for real?
JACK. You can smoke some now and sublet the rest.
PHIL. Congratulations, Don. I'm really happy for you.
JACK. Don't get maudlin, Phil.
DON. You guys having a good time?
JACK. You bet. I love eating next to the men's room.
DON. Huh? Oh, look, I'm really sorry about that . . .
PHIL. Doesn't bother me . . .
DON. See, I didn't know, Lisa did the seating . . .
JACK. No need to apologize, Big Don. I'm sure you had

48

more important things on your mind.

DON. Well, yeah . . .

JACK. You couldn't be expected to bother with these little *details.*

DON. I didn't look too stupid, did I?

JACK. No, not too stupid.

DON. Did you notice when my collar button popped off?

JACK. Actually, Big Don, I did not notice that. Actually I missed most of the ceremony, lovely as I know it must have been, actually since I was not part of the wedding party, that is the wedding party *per se,* I did not actually think it was that important for me to—

PHIL. Well, this is quite a reception. I love the, ah . . . and the *music* . . .

DON. Yeah, Lisa's parents, they're very . . . you know, they wanted a big thing.

JACK. And they're certainly getting a big thing, eh, Big Don?

DON. Ho ho.

JACK. Yep. (*Pause.*) So, Donerooney, this is the day for you, huh. Tying that wacky old knot. Strolling down that goofy aisle of matrimony. Setting down to a big heap o' domestic bliss.

DON. Well, I hope so.

JACK. You're gonna love it, kid. Take it from me. Be fruitful and multiply.

PHIL. She's a lovely girl, Don.

DON. Huh?

PHIL. Lisa.

DON. Well, thanks.

JACK. Big Don, let me ask you something.

DON. Shoot.

JACK. You and the little woman, you're off on a honeymoon?

DON. Uh-huh.

JACK. So what's happening with your apartment while you're away?

DON. My folks are gonna stay there.

JACK. Well, isn't that thoughtful.

DON. Did you—

JACK. Me? Don't concern yourself with me. (*Pause.*)

PHIL. Well, it's hard to believe.

JACK. What?

PHIL. That we're here, all three of us. And that we've known each other, all these years. I mean we were younger, we didn't know what we were gonna do, or what was gonna happen, and now we're all older, you've got a kid, you're getting married . . . just think.

JACK. It's not that difficult a concept, Phil.

PHIL. I hope you and Lisa will be very happy together, Don.

DON. I don't see why not.

JACK. You can always get a divorce. (*Phil looks at him.*) What I say?

PHIL. He just got *married*, Jack.

JACK. I'm aware of that. I'm just saying it's an option. It's something to take into account. Right, Don?

DON. Well, I suppose it's always a possibility.

JACK. You see? It's a possibility. (*Pause.*) You wanna smoke that reefer now?

DON. You have it. I'm not really supposed to.

JACK. Oh?

DON. I sort of promised myself. It's no big deal.

JACK. No, certainly not.

DON. It's something I've been wanting to do.

JACK. By all means.

DON. Anyway they're just as bad as cigarettes.

JACK. Yet another significant consideration. When do you learn to tie your shoes?

DON. I'm wearing slip-ons.

JACK. The bedrock of a lasting marriage.

DON. (*Casually.*) Fuck you, Jack.

JACK. Does that mean you don't love me anymore?

DON. Not if you're gonna talk like that.

JACK. I thought we were discussing footwear. (*Pause.*)

DON. Jack, I'm sorry.

JACK. About what?

DON. I don't know.

JACK. Then why did you say it?

DON. I don't know, I thought . . . I don't know, I'm just

50

sorry.

JACK. You know what I always like about you, Don? You're so fucking eager to please. It's really pathetic. (*Pause.*) In a zany kind of way. (*Pause.*)

DON. I better go. I have to wheel my aunt around.

JACK. Go get her, cowboy.

DON. I'm glad you guys came. I am. Listen, when I get back—

JACK. You know it.

PHIL. Great.

DON. Okay. Rest easy. (*He exits. Pause.*)

JACK. Don of the Living Dead.

PHIL. Huh?

JACK. Guy's walking around like a fucking *zombie*.

PHIL. He looked all right to me.

JACK. Did he? Did he now?

PHIL. He looked happy.

JACK. Phil, and I hate to be the one to break this to you, but you're hopelessly out of date. Happiness, that was the sixties. Paisley trousers, peace marches, that whole thing. This is the modern world. It's kinda young, kinda kooky, kinda—

PHIL. Why don't you shut the fuck up. I'm sick of you and your miserable sarcastic bullshit. (*Pause.*) I'm gonna go dance the Hokey-Pokey.

JACK. Phil.

PHIL. Don't say it.

JACK. No, Phil, wait, come here. Look at me, come on.

PHIL. What?

JACK. This is bad. This is all wrong. I'm kidding, doesn't anybody know I'm kidding? Look at me, do I look serious?

PHIL. No.

JACK. No, of course not, no, how long do we know each other?

PHIL. A long time.

JACK. Since we were midgets, Phil. Now, all right, we have our differences, our points of *view*, but basically—

PHIL. Yeah.

JACK. Basically we're friends, you and me, friends, yes?

PHIL. We're friends.

JACK. That's right we are, and we're not gonna forget that cause of a little—I'm not. I swear *I'm* not. I know what's right, Phil, I do, and I know what's wrong, and . . . so . . . so . . . don't be mad at me, okay?
PHIL. I'm not mad at you.
JACK. You're not? I knew it Phil, you big hunk, I love you. (*He hugs Phil. Pause.*) So . . . can I have the apartment? (*Phil looks at him. Pause. He turns to go.*) Phil . . . (*Phil starts off.*) Hey, Phil . . . Phil! What is that supposed to be, an answer? I'm *talking* to you, Phil! (*Phil keeps walking.*) Oh yeah? Then *fuck* you. I will *make* my arrangements. And you know *nothing*. Live with *that*. (*Phil exits.*) You fucking . . . *child.* (*Pause. He sits. Silence. Carla enters in evening dress. She stands next to Jack.*)
CARLA. Howdy stranger.
JACK. Hi.
CARLA. Guess what.
JACK. What.
CARLA. I'm having a *good* time. How about you? (*Jack nods.*) Ah, the silent type. I like that in a fella. Wanna get married?
JACK. Sure. (*She sits.*)
CARLA. I'm a little drunk.
JACK. No.
CARLA. Yeah. I'm just gonna close my eyes a sec.
JACK. You do that.
CARLA. I will. (*She leans her head on his shoulder.*) Did I tell you how nice you look?
JACK. No.
CARLA. Well, I'm going to. You look very nice. I was watching you sit here saying how nice he can look. Why does he look so nice. (*She smiles to herself. Pause.*)
JACK. We should get going.
CARLA. Mmmm.
JACK. The sitter's waiting.
CARLA. Home home. Home with you. Know what I'm thinking?
JACK. Uh-uh.
CARLA. You're not the worst man in the world.
JACK. I'm not, huh?

52

CARLA. No you're not. I'm afraid you're just not. (*Pause.*)
But you'd like to be . . . (*She rests against his shoulder with her eyes closed. Jack looks out front. Fade out.*)

END.

PROPERTY LIST

Scene 1

Joint
Headphones
Bottles
Clothes
Books

Scene 2

Bed
Coats

Scene 3

Bench
Joint
Empty bottle of imported beer
Headphones

Scene 4

Table
Check

Scene 5

Joint
Paperback
Alarm clock
Bell
Piece of paper

Scene 6

Bench
Child's toy

Scene 7

Lit candle in a saucer

Scene 8

Panties

Scene 9

Round banquet table
Napkins
Glasses
Half-eaten dinners
Row of soda-filled glasses
Sugar
Gargantuan joint

NEW PLAYS

★ **THE CREDEAUX CANVAS by Keith Bunin.** A forged painting leads to tragedy among friends. "There is that moment between adolescence and middle age when being disaffected looks attractive. Witness the enduring appeal of Prince Hamlet, Jake Barnes and James Dean, on the stage, page and screen. Or, more immediately, take a look at the lithe young things in THE CREDEAUX CANVAS..." –*NY Times.* "THE CREDEAUX CANVAS is the third recent play about painters...it turned out to be the best of the lot, better even than most plays about non-painters." –*NY Magazine.* [2M, 2W] ISBN: 0-8222-1838-0

★ **THE DIARY OF ANNE FRANK by Frances Goodrich and Albert Hackett, newly adapted by Wendy Kesselman.** A transcendently powerful new adaptation in which Anne Frank emerges from history a living, lyrical, intensely gifted young girl. "Undeniably moving. It shatters the heart. The evening never lets us forget the inhuman darkness waiting to claim its incandescently human heroine." –*NY Times.* "A sensitive, stirring and thoroughly engaging new adaptation." –*NY Newsday.* "A powerful new version that moves the audience to gasps, then tears." –*A.P.* "One of the year's ten best." – *Time Magazine.* [5M, 5W, 3 extras] ISBN: 0-8222-1718-X

★ **THE BOOK OF LIZ by David Sedaris and Amy Sedaris.** Sister Elizabeth Donderstock makes the cheese balls that support her religious community, but feeling unappreciated among the Squeamish, she decides to try her luck in the outside world. "...[a] delightfully off-key, off-color hymn to clichés we all live by, whether we know it or not." –*NY Times.* "Good-natured, goofy and frequently hilarious..." –*NY Newsday.* "...[THE BOOK OF LIZ] may well be the world's first Amish picaresque...hilarious..." –*Village Voice.* [2M, 2W (doubling, flexible casting to 8M, 7W)] ISBN: 0-8222-1827-5

★ **JAR THE FLOOR by Cheryl L. West.** A quartet of black women spanning four generations makes up this hilarious and heartwarming dramatic comedy. "...a moving and hilarious account of a black family sparring in a Chicago suburb..." –*NY Magazine.* "...heart-to-heart confrontations and surprising revelations...first-rate..." –*NY Daily News.* "...unpretentious good feelings...bubble through West's loving and humorous play..." –*Star-Ledger.* "...one of the wisest plays I've seen in ages...[from] a master playwright." –*USA Today.* [5W] ISBN: 0-8222-1809-7

★ **THIEF RIVER by Lee Blessing.** Love between two men over decades is explored in this incisive portrait of coming to terms with who you are. "Mr. Blessing unspools the plot ingeniously, skipping back and forth in time as the details require...an absorbing evening." –*NY Times.* "...wistful and sweet-spirited..." –*Variety.* [6M] ISBN: 0-8222-1839-9

★ **THE BEGINNING OF AUGUST by Tom Donaghy.** When Jackie's wife abruptly and mysteriously leaves him and their infant daughter, a pungently comic reevaluation of suburban life ensues. "Donaghy holds a cracked mirror up to the contemporary American family, anatomizing its frailties and miscommunications in fractured language that can be both funny and poignant." –*The Philadelphia Inquirer.* "...[A] sharp, eccentric new comedy. Pungently funny...fresh and precise..." –*LA Times.* [3M, 2W] ISBN: 0-8222-1786-4

★ **OUTSTANDING MEN'S MONOLOGUES 2001–2002 and OUTSTANDING WOMEN'S MONOLOGUES 2001–2002 edited by Craig Pospisil.** Drawn exclusively from Dramatists Play Service publications, these collections for actors feature over fifty monologues each and include an enormous range of voices, subject matter and characters. MEN'S ISBN: 0-8222-1821-6 WOMEN'S ISBN: 0-8222-1822-4

DRAMATISTS PLAY SERVICE, INC.
440 Park Avenue South, New York, NY 10016 212-683-8960 Fax 212-213-1539
postmaster@dramatists.com www.dramatists.com

NEW PLAYS

★ **A LESSON BEFORE DYING by Romulus Linney, based on the novel by Ernest J. Gaines.** An innocent young man is condemned to death in backwoods Louisiana and must learn to die with dignity. "The story's wrenching power lies not in its outrage but in the almost inexplicable grace the characters must muster as their only resistance to being treated like lesser beings." –*The New Yorker.* "Irresistible momentum and a cathartic explosion...a powerful inevitability." –*NY Times.* [5M, 2W] ISBN: 0-8222-1785-6

★ **BOOM TOWN by Jeff Daniels.** A searing drama mixing small-town love, politics and the consequences of betrayal. "...a brutally honest, contemporary foray into classic themes, exploring what moves people to lie, cheat, love and dream. By BOOM TOWN's climactic end there are no secrets, only bare truth." –*Oakland Press.* "...some of the most electrifying writing Daniels has ever done..." –*Ann Arbor News.* [2M, 1W] ISBN: 0-8222-1760-0

★ **INCORRUPTIBLE by Michael Hollinger.** When a motley order of medieval monks learns their patron saint no longer works miracles, a larcenous, one-eyed minstrel shows them an outrageous new way to pay old debts. "A lightning-fast farce, rich in both verbal and physical humor." –*American Theatre.* "Everything fits snugly in this funny, endearing black comedy...an artful blend of the mock-formal and the anachronistically breezy...A piece of remarkably dexterous craftsmanship." –*Philadelphia Inquirer.* "A farcical romp, scintillating and irreverent." –*Philadelphia Weekly.* [5M, 3W] ISBN: 0-8222-1787-2

★ **CELLINI by John Patrick Shanley.** Chronicles the life of the original "Renaissance Man," Benvenuto Cellini, the sixteenth-century Italian sculptor and man-about-town. Adapted from the autobiography of Benvenuto Cellini, translated by J. Addington Symonds. "[Shanley] has created a convincing Cellini, not neglecting his dark side, and a trim, vigorous, fast-moving show." –*BackStage.* "Very entertaining...With brave purpose, the narrative undermines chronology before untangling it...touching and funny..." –*NY Times.* [7M, 2W (doubling)] ISBN: 0-8222-1808-9

★ **PRAYING FOR RAIN by Robert Vaughan.** Examines a burst of fatal violence and its aftermath in a suburban high school. "Thought provoking and compelling." –*Denver Post.* "Vaughan's powerful drama offers hope and possibilities." –*Theatre.com.* "[The play] doesn't put forth compact, tidy answers to the problem of youth violence. What it does offer is a compelling exploration of the forces that influence an individual's choices, and of the proverbial lifelines—be they familial, communal, religious or political—that tragically slacken when society gives in to apathy, fear and self-doubt..." –*Westword.* "...a symphony of anger..." –*Gazette Telegraph.* [4M, 3W] ISBN: 0-8222-1807-0

★ **GOD'S MAN IN TEXAS by David Rambo.** When a young pastor takes over one of the most prestigious Baptist churches from a rip-roaring old preacher-entrepreneur, all hell breaks loose. "...the pick of the litter of all the works at the Humana Festival..." –*Providence Journal.* "...a wealth of both drama and comedy in the struggle for power..." –*LA Times.* "...the first act is so funny...deepens in the second act into a sobering portrait of fear, hope and self-delusion..." –*Columbus Dispatch.* [3M] ISBN: 0-8222-1801-1

★ **JESUS HOPPED THE 'A' TRAIN by Stephen Adly Guirgis.** A probing, intense portrait of lives behind bars at Rikers Island. "...fire-breathing...whenever it appears that JESUS is settling into familiar territory, it slides right beneath expectations into another, fresher direction. It has the courage of its intellectual restlessness...[JESUS HOPPED THE 'A' TRAIN] has been written in flame." –*NY Times.* [4M, 1W] ISBN: 0-8222-1799-6

DRAMATISTS PLAY SERVICE, INC.
440 Park Avenue South, New York, NY 10016 212-683-8960 Fax 212-213-1539
postmaster@dramatists.com www.dramatists.com

NEW PLAYS

★ **THE CIDER HOUSE RULES, PARTS 1 & 2 by Peter Parnell, adapted from the novel by John Irving.** Spanning eight decades of American life, this adaptation from the Irving novel tells the story of Dr. Wilbur Larch, founder of the St. Cloud's, Maine orphanage and hospital, and of the complex father-son relationship he develops with the young orphan Homer Wells. "...luxurious digressions, confident pacing...an enterprise of scope and vigor..." *–NY Times.* "...The fact that I can't wait to see Part 2 only begins to suggest just how good it is..." *–NY Daily News.* "...engrossing...an odyssey that has only one major shortcoming: It comes to an end." *–Seattle Times.* "...outstanding...captures the humor, the humility...of Irving's 588-page novel..." *–Seattle Post-Intelligencer.* [9M, 10W, doubling, flexible casting] PART 1 ISBN: 0-8222-1725-2 PART 2 ISBN: 0-8222-1726-0

★ **TEN UNKNOWNS by Jon Robin Baitz.** An iconoclastic American painter in his seventies has his life turned upside down by an art dealer and his ex-boyfriend. "...breadth and complexity...a sweet and delicate harmony rises from the four cast members...Mr. Baitz is without peer among his contemporaries in creating dialogue that spontaneously conveys a character's social context and moral limitations..." *–NY Times.* "...darkly funny, brilliantly desperate comedy...TEN UNKNOWNS vibrates with vital voices." *–NY Post.* [3M, 1W] ISBN: 0-8222-1826-7

★ **BOOK OF DAYS by Lanford Wilson.** A small-town actress playing St. Joan struggles to expose a murder. "...[Wilson's] best work since *Fifth of July*...An intriguing, prismatic and thoroughly engrossing depiction of contemporary small-town life with a murder mystery at its core...a splendid evening of theater..." *–Variety.* "...fascinating...a densely populated, unpredictable little world." *–St. Louis Post-Dispatch.* [6M, 5W] ISBN: 0-8222-1767-8

★ **THE SYRINGA TREE by Pamela Gien.** Winner of the 2001 Obie Award. A breathtakingly beautiful tale of growing up white in apartheid South Africa. "Instantly engaging, exotic, complex, deeply shocking...a thoroughly persuasive transport to a time and a place...stun[s] with the power of a gut punch..." *–NY Times.* "Astonishing...affecting ...[with] a dramatic and heartbreaking conclusion...A deceptive sweet simplicity haunts THE SYRINGA TREE..." *–A.P.* [1W (or flexible cast)] ISBN: 0-8222-1792-9

★ **COYOTE ON A FENCE by Bruce Graham.** An emotionally riveting look at capital punishment. "The language is as precise as it is profane, provoking both troubling thought and the occasional cheerful laugh...will change you a little before it lets go of you." *–Cincinnati CityBeat.* "...excellent theater in every way..." *–Philadelphia City Paper.* [3M, 1W] ISBN: 0-8222-1738-4

★ **THE PLAY ABOUT THE BABY by Edward Albee.** Concerns a young couple who have just had a baby and the strange turn of events that transpire when they are visited by an older man and woman. "An invaluable self-portrait of sorts from one of the few genuinely great living American dramatists...rockets into that special corner of theater heaven where words shoot off like fireworks into dazzling patterns and hues." *–NY Times.* "An exhilarating, wicked...emotional terrorism." *–NY Newsday.* [2M, 2W] ISBN: 0-8222-1814-3

★ **FORCE CONTINUUM by Kia Corthron.** Tensions among black and white police officers and the neighborhoods they serve form the backdrop of this discomfiting look at life in the inner city. "The creator of this intense...new play is a singular voice among American playwrights...exceptionally eloquent..." *–NY Times.* "...a rich subject and a wise attitude." *–NY Post.* [6M, 2W, 1 boy] ISBN: 0-8222-1817-8

DRAMATISTS PLAY SERVICE, INC.
440 Park Avenue South, New York, NY 10016 212-683-8960 Fax 212-213-1539
postmaster@dramatists.com www.dramatists.com